# A Beginners Guide to Apple Watch Series 2 and WatchOS 3

### By Scott La Counte

# Table of Contents

# Introduction

The Apple Watch is like nothing Apple has ever offered; you know how to use an iPhone; you know how to use an iPad; you may even know how to use a Mac. But an Apple Watch will probably confuse you a little…at first. It's really not hard to figure out, but there is a learning curve. This book will make using it as easy as possible.

Whether you bought the watch and want to learn how to use it, or you're thinking about making the purchase and want to see what it is about, then this guide is for you! It will cover the basics, how to customize it, popular accessories and apps available, and everything else you need to know to get the most from the device.

# How Does It Stack Up

Before seeing how the watch works, let's look at what makes it different from other smart watches on the market.

While it might seem like Apple invented the smart watch, there's actually several that came before it—for a significantly cheaper price. So why Apple Watch? In a nutshell, Apple didn't set the bar...they are the bar. In terms of smart watches, there's nothing that comes close to what Apple has built. Its menus are fluid, it's sleek, and, like other Apple products, it just works. But let's take a moment and look at how the other watches stack up against the Apple Watch.

## Android Wear

If you have an Android phone, then Android Wear is the official watch for you. Apple Watch will not be supported by Android. Most Android Wear watches are $200 to $300 dollars—though there are several cheaper options in the sub-$50 range...but they are cheaper for a reason—they don't work like they are promised to. Most Android watches have batteries that last a day...like the Apple Watch; and most, like the Apple Watch have sensors to track health and fitness. There are also plenty of apps to load onto your watch. So why is Apple Watch better than Android Wear? Opinions obviously vary, but many feel that Apple Apps work smoother and everything is more fluid. Unlike Android, Apple screens their apps to make sure apps that don't really do anything don't get on the app store. It should also be noted that WatchOS (Apple's operating system) is built for one watch; Android's Watch OS is customized for each watch, and some manufactures don't put the effort into that customization that's needed to make the watch great. Some Android Watches are supported in some capacity on the iPhone, but not all.

## Pebble

In terms of price, Pebble is the best watch for your money. The basic version starts at $99.99 and a color model is coming soon. The Pebble watch is also one of the few watches compatible with both Android and iPhone smartphones. The Pebble is not a bad watch, but it is a limited one. There is no touchscreen, graphics are subpar, and notifications are not as fluid as Apple Watch. It also won't win any fashion awards.

## Windows Band

Windows also has a watch called the Windows Band. Calling it a watch is a bit of a stretch, however. While it does tell time, it's more of a high-end fitness band. At $199, most people will be left wondering why not just pay a little more for an Apple Watch or a little less for a Fibit or Jawbone (both of which cost about $120).

# Different Models

If you haven't already bought the band, below is a quick rundown of all the different models.

The Apple Watch comes in four different models:

*Apple Watch Series 1 (starting at $269 for 38mm; $299 for 42mm)* – The cheapest Apple Watch is made of anodized aluminum that Apple claims is 60% stronger than standard aluminum (aluminum is also the medal used for the Apple iPhone). The touchscreen is made of aluminosilicate glass that's resistant to scratches.

*Apple Watch Series 2 (starting at $369 for the 38mm; $399 for the 42mm)* – Same as the series one, but with built-in GPS and water resistant up to 50m.

*Apple Watch Series 2, Stainless Steel (starting at $549 for 38mm; $599 for 42mm)* – made of 316L stainless steel that is less susceptible to scratches and corrosion. The touchscreen is sapphire crystal (perhaps the strongest screen on the market today).

*Apple Watch Edition Series 2 (starting at $1,249 for 38mm; $1,299 for 42mm)* – Jaws dropped when Apple announced its most expensive Apple Watch, which goes all the way up to $17,000 in price. The watch was made of 18-karat yellow or rose gold, which Apple says is twice as hard as standard gold. The cheapest models came with a sports band; if you wanted a leather band, then you needed to pay a few thousand more. Apple appears to have thought differently for series two, by introducing it's most expensive line for several thousand less. This time around, the band is made of a ceramic case.

Which band is right for you? Unless you have an itching to spend 1k+ for a watch, then you are probably considering the Sports or steel model. What's the difference? In terms of wear and tear, both watches will hold up pretty well; every watch—even the more expensive ones—have the same hardware. The steel and Edition models both have a stronger display that is slightly more scratch-resistant.

Unlike the iPhone or iPad, you aren't paying more for more memory—you are paying for the finish—so it's really a question of taste. The steel watch is slick, smooth and shiny. If you can afford it and want something a little classier, then the steel watch is a good option.

If you are trying to decide between the series one and series two, it really comes down to how you will use it. If you're a swimmer and want to use your watch in the pool, then you definitely want the series 2; the GPS on series 2 is also great for fitness and tracking where you go when your phone isn't next to you. Series 1 is still an excellent watch, however.

Also, if you already have the watch and don't like the band that you like, you are able to return the band (even if it's opened) to any Apple store within 14 days for a band of equal value. (Note: this offer will not necessarily run forever, so check with your local store before going in for an exchange.)

# Quick Overview of the Watch

When you think about the watch, you might have certain expectations—perhaps it's watching Netflix from your wrist or FaceTime with your friends. So before continuing to how the watch works, let me cover really quickly the major things the watch cannot do (that some people think it can):

## Things the Apple Watch won't do…

- Play videos.
- Type messages (there is no onboard keyboard…just a microphone).
- Play games — while Apple Watch games do exist, the watch is a companion to the phone, and meant for viewing short messages…not playing games. So yes, you can play games, but this is not what you want to get to meet your gaming needs.
- Sync with non-Apple phones; the Apple Watch will not work with any phone but iPhone.
- Work with older phones; the Apple Watch is for iPhone 5 and up
- Work with traditional headphones; there's no audio input on the Apple Watch; it does work with Bluetooth headphones, but these are not included with the watch.
- Take a photo; you can view photos on the watch—you can even use it as an external viewfinder to take a photo on your iPhone—but the watch has no built in camera.

## Apple Watch Without An iPhone Nearby

To be entirely clear, you must own an iPhone to use the Apple Watch. The watch is not compatible with Android or any other smart phone. But you don't have to take your iPhone everywhere to use the watch. Here are some of the things you can do if you don't have your phone nearby:

- Set the time.
- Play music (you can put up to 2 GB of songs on your watch…to put it another way, that's about 500 songs).
- Track your run / exercise — it will keep a record of things like calories burned, heart rate, and distance / pace, and then sync it to your phone when you have it nearby again.

- Track your standing time and steps.
- See your photos—75 MB is reserved for photos.
- Read, delete and flag email that has come in.
- Use the alarm, stopwatch, and timer.
- Use passbook to show tickets (like airplane or concert ticket).
- Use ApplePay to buy things.

And here's what you can do if you don't have your phone, but you do have Wi-Fi:

- Send and receive text message, and use digital touch messages (i.e. drawing and tapping patterns to send as a message).
- Use Siri.

A few other things you might need to know about the watch…

- It takes about two hours to fully charge your Apple Watch.
- It takes your iPhone's battery…kind of; because the watch talks to your phone, your phone's battery will be used. It's not significant, but it's enough that you might notice 30 minutes to an hour of usage gone by the end of the day that used to be there.
- There's a feature on the device called "Taptic Engine"--fancy sound, right? But what is it? The taptic engine lets you receive feedback on your wrist that feels like someone is tapping you.
- You can use it as a phone…sort of. Yes, it sounds very Dick Tracy-like to get phone calls on your wrist, but don't get too excited—it's a little awkward to use; to get the most out of it, you really need to put it up or near your mouth. And the audio that comes out of the speakers is subpar at best.
- It tells time! Well yes—you probably knew that. But it also tells time very precisely (within 50 milliseconds), which makes it one of the most accurate watches ever made.

# The Basics

Now it's time to get to the fun stuff: The Watch! I'm going to start with the absolute basics, so if you are comfortable with the easy stuff, then jump ahead.

## Setting up Your Phone for the First Time

Because the Apple Watch has no keyboards, setup is a bit unusual compared to other Apple products. Setup for the watch actually begins not with the watch, but with the iPhone.

If you aren't running iPhone iOS 10 and up, then the first thing you need to do is update your phone. You also need at least an iPhone 5—anything less will not be compatible. To see if your phone needs to be updated, go to Settings on the iPhone, then General, and finally Software Update—it will tell you if your phone is up-to-date.

Once everything is ready, put the watch on your wrist, and press and hold the side button until you see the Apple Logo.

While you are waiting for the watch to start, open the Apple Watch app on your iPhone—after 10 is installed, Apple Watch will be available.

After the watch loads, you will be prompted to put your iPhone above the watch so that it appears in the camera's viewfinder on the phone screen. Follow the instructions on your phone: you will be asked to pick your language, watch orientation, and passcode. You'll be able to change all this later.

*NOTE TO USERS UPDATING: If you are updating your iPhone and Watch from a previous OS, there's a chance you will have to reformat your watch to get it to sync. If that happens, then from your watch you need to go to Settings / General / Reset; next tap Erase All Content and Settings.*

When prompted, position your iPhone so that Apple Watch appears in the camera viewfinder on the iPhone screen. Follow the instructions on iPhone and Apple Watch to finish setup. During setup, you'll choose your language, watch orientation, and passcode. The entire setup will take several minutes—but don't worry: this is a one-time thing.

If your watch is new, then it should be charged; if you need to charge it, refer to the section in this book on Charging.

There are a lot of settings in the Apple Watch app on your iPhone, and I'll refer back to them as the book goes on.

It's also worth going to the Settings app from your Apple Watch and just seeing what's there and becoming familiar with it.

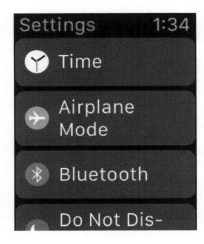

# Power on, Wake, and Unlock

To turn your watch on, press and hold the side button until the Apple logo appears; to turn it off press and hold the side button until a slider appears telling you to drag it to the right to power off.

Taking your phone off standby is the most seamless thing you'll do—just lift your wrist! How's that for easy? Turning standby back on is just as simple—put your wrist down.

If you lift your wrist and standby doesn't turn off, then it's possible that you changed a setting. Open the Setting button on the home screen of your watch (it looks just like the one on your phone except it's round, and then go to General and Orientation—make sure Orientation is set to the wrist that you wear—if you are wearing it on your right hand and Orientation is set to left hand, for example, then change it. The other thing that might have happened is your battery has drained.

When you lift your wrist, the watch will either show your watch face (i.e. time) or the last app opened. By default it shows the watch face, but if you want it to go to your last activity, then go to Settings, then General, and finally Activate on Wrist Raise—once you tap this, pick Resume Previous Activity.

You also have the ability to unlock the watch with your phone using a Passcode. This is a great feature if you take your watch off a lock. It doesn't mean you need to put in a passcode every time you look at the time—it only needs it when the watch is off your wrist or being worn too loosely. The Passcode can be the same as the phone, but it's recommended that the code is different. To activate Passcode, go to Settings from your watch's home screen, and then scroll down until you see Passcode, then tap it. Tap turn on Unlock with iPhone. If you ever want to change it, just follow the same steps, but pick Change Passcode.

If you ever forget your passcode, then unpair it from the iPhone and erase all the settings.

You can also lock the watch manually. To do this, press and hold the side button; when the sliders appear, slide the Lock Device option to the right.

## Adjusting Text Size, Brightness, Sounds, and Haptics

For this section, we will be spending all of our time in the Settings portion of the watch, so head to it by going to your home screen and tapping on the Settings icon.

The Apple Watch is probably smaller than you're used to when reading messages, emails, news, etc.; if it's too small then you can make text larger by going to Brightness and Text Size, tap Text Size and then use the Digital Crown knob to increase or decrease it. You can also check or uncheck making the text boldface (Note: Before boldface is in place the watch will need to be reset.).

From this same menu, you can adjust how bright the watch is.

If you don't like the default sounds on your watch, then go to Sounds & Haptics from the Settings menu.  Use your Digital Crown knob to adjust how loud it gets. You can also mute sounds by switching the Mute button from Off to On (Note: muting does not turn off sound on alarms).

Like many things on the Apple Watch, there are a lot of things that can be done quickly with Gestures; that's true with sound. To quickly mute sounds, put the palm of your hand over the watch and hold it there for three seconds; you'll feel a tap when you can uncover. For this to work, however, you must first enable it from your phone by opening the Apple Watch app, going to Sounds & Haptics, and finally cover to mute.

For some notifications, you will get a tap on your wrist, which you may love or hate. If you hate it, then go back to the previous menu.  Next, go to the Haptic button under Ringer. You can use the Digital Crown to adjust the haptic intensity.

# Charge the Apple Watch

Charging your watch is very simple; it might be a little strange at first, because the charger is magnetic and doesn't plug into the watch — rather it snaps into the back. Make sure you use the charger case that came with your device — using any other might overcharge the device, which will drain the battery quickly. The only other approved chargers are the ones that come with your iPhone or iPad.

It takes about two hours to fully charge the watch.

If you want to know how much time is needed for a full charge, swipe up from the watch face, which brings up Glances, and then swipe to the Battery glance.

When the watch has less than 10% power left, it will automatically go into a Power Reserve mode — in this mode, the watch will show the time, but other apps won't be available. You can also manually turn Power Reserve on by pressing the side button for three seconds until the Power menu comes up, then swiping Power Reserve.

You can see how much time you have left in your battery reserve at any time by swiping up from the watch face to bring up Glances, then swiping to Power

Reserve. You can also use the Apple Watch app on your iPhone to see the last time you charged it.

# Status Icons

As you use the watch, there are a couple of indicators that will appear that you should be aware of. They are listed below:

●

You have an unread notification such as an email.

⚡

The Apple Watch is charging.

🔒

The Apple Watch is locked and needs a passcode to use.

🌙

Your watch is in "Do Not Disturb" mode and will not make any sounds or light up until enabled again; alarms, however, will still work.

✈

The Apple Watch is in Airplane mode and only non-wireless features work — Bluetooth and Wi-Fi are not turned on.

📵

Your watch is no longer paired with your phone.

There's wireless activity happening or some other kind of active event—an app loading for example.

# Gestures and Shortcuts

With such a limited space, Apple really made use of something called Gestures. Gestures is essentially your watch doing different things based on how you touch or swipe the watch. Below is a quick overview of the gestures and shortcuts that let you do what you need to do quickly.

The one shortcut you will use the most is the Digital Crown; pressing it will always get you back to the home screen. It's like the square button on your iPhone.

## Force Touch

Force Touch measures not just what you are touching, but how hard you are touching it. On your watch/clock screen, pressing a little harder on the screen will let you change the watch face. In apps, Force Touch is used a bit like right clicking on a computer--it brings up options.

## Notifications

When you swipe down from the top of your watch, you bring up recent notifications (things like emails and messages), which you may have missed when they first came in.

## Zooming

You may be used to pinching and zooming on your iPhone and iPad; be prepared to be disappointed...on a smaller screen this method just doesn't work. In its place is the digital crown, which can be used to zoom in and out by turning the knob. You can use it to magnify things like photos and maps.

## Turning off the Screen

There's no physical button to turn off the Apple Watch. To turn the screen off you can either put your hand down, or cover the watch with your hand. You can also silence alarms by covering your hand over the screen.

## Launching Siri

There are two quick ways to launch Siri: one, press and hold the Digital Crown; two, lift up your wrist and say "Hey Siri"--no buttons are required.

## Locate your iPhone

If you can't find your iPhone, you can quickly ping it with your watch to see if it's nearby. Go to your watch face, swipe up to bring up Glances, swipe to the Settings glance, and then tap the button under Pink iPhone.

This will make your phone start beeping (Note: for this to work you must enable Find My iPhone from iCloud).

## Airplane Mode

Most airlines will let you leave your watch turned on while you're flying, but they will want it in airplane mode (which turns off settings that might interfere with the plane).

To put the watch in Airplane Mode, go to your watch face, swipe up from the bottom to bring up Glances, and go to the Settings glance, then tap the button that looks like an airplane. Repeat the step to turn the mode off.

If you'd like the watch to go in Airplane Mode whenever your phone does, then go to the Apple Watch app, tap My Watch, then tap Airplane Mode and turn on

Mirror iPhone. Repeat the step to disable.

# Apple Pay

To use Apple Pay, double tap the side button; it will come up with your credit card and tell you to put it near the reader (your phone does not need to be nearby); once it is by the reader you enter your passcode. Worried about someone taking your phone and using your credit card? It won't work when it's taken off your wrist.

When you get to a reader that supports Apple Pay, simply double tap the side button. If you want to use a different credit card, swipe to the left. When you find the card you want, turn it to face the reader. When the transactions goes through, you'll hear a beep and you'll feel a tap—this alerts you to the fact that the transaction is complete.

Before you can use Apple Pay, however, you need to set it up. This is done on the iPhone. From your iPhone, tap the Apple Watch app, and then scroll to "Add Credit or Debit Card," and then tap it. You can either use a card on file with iTunes or add a new card. In either case you'll have to add your security number (or the full number if you are adding a new card); depending on the card, you may need to verify with another step, which is usually a text message with a code from your bank. When you get the code, just tap Verify and enter it. You're all set to use your watch to buy things!

# Handoff between the Apple Watch and iPhone

Handoff lets you toggle between your watch and your phone without losing your place. If you are reading an email on your watch, and want to reply on your phone, then go to your phone; on the standby screen you will see an icon in the lower left corner; swipe up over that icon and the email you were reading on your watch is now on your phone. (Note: For this to work, your phone does need to be near your watch.)

As of this writing, Handoff supports the following apps: Mail, Maps, Messages, Phone, Reminders, Calendar, and Siri.

You can turn Handoff on and off by opening the Apple Watch app on your iPhone, going to My Watch, then tapping on General and Enable Handoff.

# Arranging Icons

Arranging icons on the watch isn't that much different from arranging them on your iPhone or iPad. To start, go to your home screen, then touch and hold an app icon; you can now drag it to a new location.

To install a new app, open the Apple Watch app from your iPhone (Note: you have to use your iPhone to install apps), and then tap the App Store to find apps for the Apple Watch. Once you download them from your phone, you'll see a message on your watch asking if you want to install them. Just tap yes and you are done. When you are on the normal app store, you'll see a little round icon and "Offers Apple Watch App" if it's an app with a companion app for the watch.

The watch doesn't have as much room as your phone, so you might run out of space. To view how much storage is being used by an app, go to the Apple Watch app on the iPhone, then tap on My Watch, then go to General and Usage. Finally, view the storage being used by each app.

If you would like to remove an app, go to the home screen on the watch, then tap and hold the app you want to remove; when an X appears over the app, tap it. It will remain installed on your iPhone unless you remove it from there as well. Apps that were installed by Apple (such as the Settings button) cannot be removed.

If you find the screen a bit to small for rearranging icons, then you can also do it right from your iPhone; just open the Apple Watch app, tap the My Watch tab, and tap Layout. You rearrange the icons just as you would on your watch.

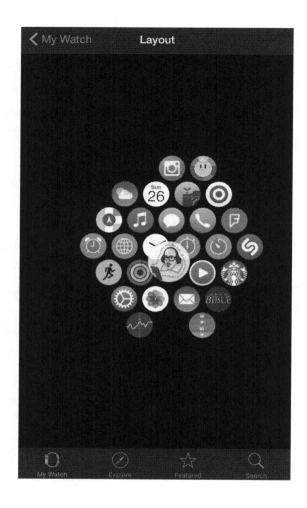

## Dock It

Previous versions of WatchOS enabled you to quickly contact your friends and family when you pressed the side button; that's changed with WatchOS 3. The side button is now used to toggle between the apps you use the most.

# SOS

SOS is another feature new to WatchOS 3. SOS allows your Watch to call local emergency services to tell them your location; this is obviously something you only use in an emergency--it's not something try out just to see how it works! To enable it, hold the side button for 3 seconds, and then swipe SOS.

# Breathe

Breathe is a new app on the WatchOS 3 home screen. It's a free relaxation app designed to help calm your body after a workout or stressful day at work.

# Features

## Watch Faces

The Apple Watch has dozens of different faces to pick from—from traditional to modern to even a cute Mickey Mouse (and Minnie Mouse on OS 3). To change the watch's face, place your finger firmly over the current face for three seconds. The face will zoom back and you can swipe back and forth across your watch's screen to see different faces. Some watches you can customize; when that's possible you'll see a button that says Customize.

When you find the face that you want, tap it. Before tapping, however, you can also customize it by tapping the Customize button.

You'll see dots at the top of the screen to indicate how much you can change. On the first screen, scroll with the knob to see what changes (it might, for instance, change the number of numbers on the watch). When you are done, swipe across the screen to get to the next customizable screen: colors. Using the knob, you can scroll through all of the colors. Swipe again, and you'll be at a screen that lets you add the current weather, calendar, etc. You'll tap on the screen to change any of these features, but first you have to swipe the Off to On.

After you have customized the face to suit your needs, press the knob. This will bring you back to the main face screen. From here, tap the face. Your new face should now appear with all its customizations. If you added options for calendar and weather, you can now tap those options to bring up more detailed views. To bring up the more detailed view, tap your finger on the icon on the screen (e.g., to see the weather, for instance, tap the weather icon).

And remember, anytime you want to know the time anywhere else in the world, just say "Siri, what time is it in…?"

## *Watch Faces and What They Do*

Every face has different details that can be added or removed. Below is a list of the current watch faces and what you can add to them.

### Astronomy

This watch face shows you the exact position for different planets and displays day, date and time.

### Chronograph

A very precise and classic watch face that includes a stopwatch that can be activated from the watch face. The following can be adjusted: dial details and face color. You can also add the following to the face: date, moon phase, sunrise / sunset, calendar, weather, stock, activity summary, alarm, timer, battery charge, world clock.

Color

A very basic face whose primary feature is changing the colors. The following can be adjusted: Dial color. The following can be added to the face: date, moon phase, sunrise / sunset, weather, activity summary, stopwatch, timer, batter charge, world clock, your monogram.

Mickey Mouse

Featuring Mickey Mouse (now with Minnie Mouse), this is certainly the most whimsical and animated watch experience. The following can be added to the face: date, calendar, moon phase, sunrise / sunset, weather, activity summary, alarm, timer, stopwatch, battery charge, world clock, stocks.

## Modular

A very modern-looking face with lots of room to add things. The following can be adjusted: color. The following features can be added: calendar, moon phase, sunrise / sunset, weather, stocks, activity summary, alarm, timer, stopwatch, battery charge, world clock.

## Motion

This and the Mickey face are the only ones that are fully animated. You can pick between a butterfly, flower, and jellyfish. The following can be added to the face: date.

Simple

As the name implies, this is the simplest classic watch face. The following can be adjusted on the face: color of the sweep hand and the numbering of the dial. The following can be added: date, calendar, moon phase, sunrise / sunset, weather, activity summary, alarm, timer, stopwatch, battery charge, and world clock.

Solar

Bring out your inner scientist with this app, which displays the sun's position in the sky.

## Utility

A very basic and classic looking face; the following features can be changed: the color of the second hand and the numbering on the dial. The following can be added to the face: date, calendar, moon phase, sunrise / sunset, weather, activity summary, alarm, timer, stopwatch, batter charge, world clock, stock.

## X-Large

X-Large is the most simplistic modern face — it's also the boldest looking. The following can be adjusted: color.

## Notifications

Notifications are things that an app will send to keep you informed. They can be everything from meeting invites to exercise reminders — there's dozens of different ones. When you get a notification, it is displayed on your watch; if you don't read it right away, it's saved so you can refer back to it later.

If you find that you are getting far too many notifications, you can adjust it by going to the Settings app on your iPhone, then selecting Notifications. You'll see all of the apps with notifications and you can turn off the ones that you do not want.

If you want notifications, but you don't want them to make a sound, then swipe up from your watch face to go to Glances; next, go to the Settings glance, and tap Silent Mode. You'll still feel a tap, but you won't hear a noise. If you don't want the tap either, then turn on Do Not Disturb.

If you don't respond to a notification right away, then a red dot will appear at the top of your watch face. Swipe down from the watch face to read it.

If you want to delete a notification, swipe the notification to the left and then tap Clear. To clear all notifications, then tap firmly on the display and then clear all.

# Messages

To begin a new message, go to your watch's home screen by pressing the knob, tap the Message icon, and press and hold your finger firmly on the screen. After three seconds it will ask if you'd like to start a new message. From here, tap the "Add a contact"; once you pick your contact, tap "Create message."

When you receive a message, Apple Watch will tap you. Move your hand toward you and the message will appear automatically; once you put your hand down, it turns off again. Use the watch's side knob to scroll through the message. There's no reply button! So how do you reply? You have several different options, and you'll see those options under the last message.

One:

Dictation (The blue mic icon). If you'd like to send an audio message or speak your reply, then tap Reply on the message, and then tap the microphone icon. Begin speaking into the watch (note: you'll notice audio waves on the screen). When you finish, tap Done. It will ask if you want to send it as an audio reply (so the person has to listen to it) or as a text reply (so the person can see it). You can also cancel the message and start a new one.

Two:

Emojis (The blue happy face icon). You may know emojis as cute little smiley faces. On Apple Watch, these faces become animated. To get started, tap Reply, and then hit the Emoji button (the smiley face button). An animated face will appear; you can change how it looks, by moving the side knob up and down. You can also pick different gestures, by swiping across the emoji (the first you will see is a heart). When you find the one you want, tap Send.

Three:

Digital Touch (The heart with two fingers). This let's you send the person heartbeats and taps.

Four:

Scribble. As the name implies, you can tap this icon, scribble a message, and send away.

Five.

Smart replies. Apple Watch automatically detects what your message is and will try to have a generic reply that you can use to reply. Use the knob to scroll through auto replies and tap to select the reply.

If no reply is needed, then hit the Dismiss button instead of the Reply button.

If you are not getting messages on your watch, then chances are a Setting is not enabled; you can change the Message setting from the Apple Watch app on your iPhone.

## Reading and Sending Email

When you get mail, you'll also get a notification; but there's also an app for reading and managing your email. As it is on the iPhone, the email app is simply named "Mail."

To start, go to the app on your home screen and tap on it. It looks pretty bare bones, but there's a lot to it. You can scroll through your messages from within the app. To read a message, tap it.

At any time, you can continue reading the message on your iPhone, by swiping up on the Mail icon in the lower left corner of your iPhone's lock screen (Note: handoff does need to be set up, so refer to how to set up handoff in this book if you haven't already).

While Apple Watch does support HTML formats (including different fonts and font colors), it still might look a little off, so for a complex message, the iPhone is the best place to read them.

If it's a long message, you can use the Digital Crown knob to scroll through it.

When a message includes phone numbers or address, the watch will automatically recognize it and turn it into a hyperlink. Tapping on them will either bring up the Phone or Map app (depending on what the hyperlink is).

To reply to a message, you will need to use the iPhone to compose it.

## *Managing Mail*

### Flag an Email

When you are reading an email on the watch, you can press firmly on the display, and then tap Flag. You can also flag a message from your message list by swiping the message to the left, then tapping on More.

### Mark as Unread

If you want to mark a message as unread, go to your message list, swipe left, tap More, and then tap Unread.

### Delete an Email

If you want to delete a message, go to your message list, swipe left, tap More, and then tap Trash. (Note: if your email is set up to archive a message, then you'll see the Archive button instead of the Trash button.)

### Selecting the Inboxes that Appear

You may not want all of your mail to appear on your phone. Let's say you have a work email, family email, and spam email, and you only want your family email to appear. If that's the case then go to the Apple Watch app on your iPhone, tap My Watch, and then go to Mail and Include Mail. Specify which mailbox you do or do not want to appear.

### Customize Alerts

If you want to change how you are alerted when you get mail (or if you don't want alerts at all), then go to the Apple Watch app on your iPhone, and tap My Watch, then turn on Mail Alerts and Show Alerts. Sound would be alerts that make noises and Haptic is alerts that vibrate.

### Message List

If you find your email message list is simply too long, you can reduce the number of lines of the preview by going to the Apple Watch app, tapping on My Watch and then going to Mail and Message Preview; pick 2 lines of message, 1 line of message or no lines of a message.

# Siri

If you love Siri on the iPhone, you're going to love her even more on your wrist. Don't love her? Give her a second chance because she got a little bit of an upgrade.

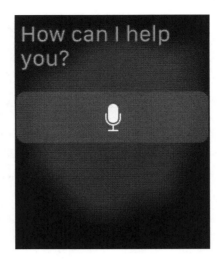

You can access Siri one of two ways (you'll quickly discover that there are multiple ways to do most tasks on the watch):

1. Press the Digital Crown knob.
2. Raise your wrist and say, "Hey, Siri" then say your request (e.g. "Hey, Siri: what's the weather in Paris?" "Hey, Siri: Who won last night's Yankee game?"); you can use Siri to open apps, set alarms, call friends—pretty much anything you can think of. With no on-board keyboard, Siri is more important than ever.

## Making Phone Calls

While you may not go out and buy and Apple Watch to get your Dick Tracy on and make phone calls from your wrist, it's certainly a nice touch...and it's pretty simple to do.

Once your watch is in sync with your iPhone, you are ready to start making and receiving calls.

If a call comes in, you can mute it by placing your hand over the watch. If you want to send it to your phone or reply with a text, then move your finger over the digital crown and scroll to the bottom.

To answer the call, use the green button; to decline the call, press the red one. It's just like getting a call on your iPhone. Your watch will use a built in microphone when you speak into it. It's not the best quality, but it gets the job done.

To make a call, you have three options:

1. Go to your home screen and tap the phone icon.
2. The other option is the easiest; that option is to use Siri. Just lift your wrist and say, "Hey, Siri—call PERSON'S NAME." If the wrong person is dialed, just hit the Hang Up button and if you do it quickly enough, the call won't go through.

# Calendar

The Calendar app calendar icon on Apple Watch shows events you've scheduled or been invited to today and for the next week. Apple Watch shows events for all calendars you use on your iPhone.

To view your calendar, open the Calendar app on your home screen; you can, also swipe up from your watch face to bring up Glances, and swipe until you get to the Calendar glance. You can also tap on the day's date on the watch face if you've added that option.

| April | | | | | | 2:44 |
|---|---|---|---|---|---|---|
| S | M | T | W | T | F | S |
| | | | 1 | 2 | 3 | 4 |
| 5 | 6 | 7 | 8 | 9 | 10 | 11 |
| 12 | 13 | 14 | 15 | 16 | 17 | 18 |
| 19 | 20 | 21 | 22 | 23 | 24 | 25 |
| 26 | 27 | 28 | 29 | 30 | | |

You can also see what's going on in your day by lifting your wrist and saying, "Siri tell me what's going on today.

To switch between the daily events and single list of events, press firmly on the display while you are in the Calendar app, then tap List or Day.

To view a different day, just go to Day view while in the Calendar app, and then swipe left to see the next day's events.

If you want to see the full month, then tap on the < in the upper left corner of the Calendar app, and then tap the monthly calendar; repeat the step to go back to Day view. When you are in Month view, any days that you have an activity will be highlighted in red.

## Adding Events

To add an event, you will need to open the Calendar app on your iPhone. If you are in the Calendar app on your watch, then a Calendar icon will appear on your iPhone's lock screen—just swipe up and it will go immediately to your Calendar.

You can have Siri add an event for you.

## Responding to Event Invites

When you get an invite to an event, it will appear as a notification; just swipe it or turn the Digital Crown knob when you see it, and then tap Accept, Maybe, or Decline.

The invite will also have the event organizer; to email the event organize, press firmly on the display while you are looking at the event details; you will be able to either send them a voice message or call them.

To adjust any of your Calendar's settings, go to the Apple Watch app on the iPhone, then tap My Watch, and finally tap Calendar.

## Reminders

If you use reminders on the iPhone, then you might be disappointed to see there is no Reminders app on the Apple Watch.

Reminders, however, is sort of there; while no app exists, if you create a reminder on your iPhone through the Reminders App, it will also remind you on your watch.

You can also create a reminder on your watch by using Siri; just lift your wrist and say "Hey Siri, set a reminder."

## Map

There are a couple of ways to use the map on your Apple Watch; the first and quickest is to swipe up from your watch face to bring up Glances and then swipe to the Map Glance. From here you'll see your current location and what's around you; you can use the Digital Touch knob to zoom in or out. To scroll/pan through the map, use your finger. If you tap the arrow in the bottom left corner, the current location will be updated.

To search the map, tap and hold your finger over the map; this will let you speak what you want to find or see your most recent locations.

You can tap any location that appears on your map to get directions to it or more information about it. You can also stick a pin in an area that you want to go. To add a pin, just touch and hold Map (not firmly) and wait for the pin to drop. If you tap the pin after it's been dropped, it will give you the address. To move the pin, just hover over a new location and drop a new pin. If you aren't sure what someone's address is, if you drop a pin near their address, you can get an approximate address.

# Directions

Turn by turn directions on the Apple Watch is one of the bigger features, and it's really simple to use.

When you get a text with an address, the address is automatically converted to a hyperlink; click on it, and a map will immediately open. You can zoom in and out of the map by turning the Digital Crown knob.

If you don't have a message with the address, then go to your watch's Home screen, tap the Maps icon; the map will appear showing your current location. To find an address, tap your finger firmly on the screen. You'll get an option to either search for the address or use one of your contacts' addresses. When you search for an address, it will give you the option to use a recently used address, or speak the address through dictation.

When the address comes up, there will be two options: driving directions and walking directions. Walking will not only change the time it will take, but also take you down paths a car cannot go. Once you make your selection by tapping, just hit the Start button.

One of the cool features about the map is the turn-by-turn direction. When it's time to make a turn, your watch will tap you to get your attention. Even more cool is if you start directions on your phone, it will also appear on your watch.

# Photos

To view photos on the Apple Watch, go to the Photos app on your watch home screen; because the watch cannot actually take photos, the photos you see will be the ones from your iPhone album. By default, the watch is set to display only your Favorites album, but you can change this.

Once the app is open, just tap the photo you want to view and use the Digital Crown knob to zoom in or out, and use your finger to pan it. Zoom all the way out to see all of your photos.

## *Pick an Album*

If you'd like to choose another album to show on your watch then open the Apple Watch app on the iPhone and tap My Watch, then go to Photos and Synced Album; pick the album you want to sync; you can also create a new album using photos from your phone.

## *Storage*

The watch does not have as much space as your phone so it's important to limit how much you store on it; to limit photo storage, open the Apple Watch app on the iPhone, tap My Watch, then go to Photos and Photo Limits.

You can see how many photos are currently on your Apple Watch by opening the Settings app from the watch's main screen, tapping General, and then About. You can also see this on your phone by opening the Apple Watch app, then tapping My Watch, General, and About.

# Camera Viewfinder

While the watch doesn't have a camera built in, it does have a pretty awesome feature that lets you use the watch as an external camera viewfinder and shutter to your iPhone camera.

For this to work, you need to make sure the watch is no more than 30 ft. from your iPhone.

To take a photo, open the Camera app on your watches home screen, then position the iPhone to frame the shot using the Apple Watch as your viewfinder. If you want to change the exposure, just tap the area you want to focus on from your Apple Watch preview; tap the shutter button on your watch. You can preview the photo on your watch, but the photo will actually be saved on the iPhone.

Next to the shutter button is a timer button; if you want to do a timed shot, tap that; the timer takes burst shots, which is great for action / sports photos.

# Music

The music app is, of course, on your home screen, but you can reach it more quickly by swiping up on your screen.

Like almost anything on the Watch, you can also play music with Siri. Just lift your wrist and say, "Hey, Siri, play Bob Dylan."

When music is playing, tap the top corner and you'll have the option to scroll through Artist, Albums, Playlist and Songs (scroll using the Digital Crown knob).

The watch automatically syncs to your phone and will play music that's on your iPhone. That's great when your phone is nearby, but sometimes you don't have your phone nearby and want to listen to music directly on your watch. You can load music to your Watch pretty easily.

## Stocks

If you'd like to monitor one or more stocks from your watch, open the Stock app; you can see details about a stock by tapping it in a list and then turning the Digital Crown to scroll.

You can also use Siri to find a stock price by saying "Hey Siri, what was the closing price for XYZ stock?"

You can also see stock as a glance by swiping up from your watch face, and swiping to the Stock glance. From here you can also add stock.

## Weather

There are a couple of ways to check weather on your watch; one of the easiest is to swipe up from your watch face to bring up Glances, and then find the Weather Glance.

If you want more detailed weather information, then go to the Weather app by opening it on the watch home screen. The Weather app will have 10-day forecast, current temperature and conditions, and chance of rain.

The Weather app is synced to your iPhone, so if you want to add or remove a city, then do it from your phone.

You can change the default city being shown on your watch by opening the Apple Watch app on your iPhone, tapping on My Watch, and then going to Weather and Default City.

To add music, connect your watch to its charger, then open the Apple Watch app on your iPhone. Next, tap Music (it's near the bottom). After that, tap "sync playlist," and choose the songs you want to add.

To play music directly from your watch, open the music app and press firmly on the screen when the app opens. This will open a new menu with four options: Shuffle, Repeat, Source, and Airplay. Select "Source." Next select Apple Watch. It will now walk you through pairing your watch with Bluetooth headsets to listen to the music.

From the previous menu, you can also select Airplay to pair your watch with an Airplay enabled speaker.

# Activity

One of the features that Apple is really promoting with the Apple Watch is Activity; one of the reasons to wear the watch, if you are to believe Apple, is to get you to move more.

The app is divided up into three fitness goals: stand up for at least one minute of every hour, hit your calorie burn goal by moving more (you can set your goal), and accumulate 30 minutes of an activity that requires movement above a brisk walk. Each of these goals make up rings; as you complete these goals, the rings begin to fill up, and by the end of the day they should ideally be full.

To get started, go to your home screen and tap the Activity app. The first time that you open the app, it will give you a very short tutorial on what the app is and how it helps you live a happier, healthier life. Once you finish the tutorial, you'll have to enter some personal information—this is for your eyes only and you only do it once. It will help ensure the app is as accurate as possible. For each section, turn the Digital Crown to enter your information.

After you've finished, you will indicate your activity level; you can change this later, so if you aren't sure, then go for lower—not higher. Next you'll see your suggested goal, which you can accept or adjust. When you are done, tap Start Moving. Your app will now be tracking you in the background. There's no need to start anything each day.

You can access the Activity app at any time by tapping on it from your home screen, but you can also get to it by swiping up from your watch face to see it in your Glances. The first thing you'll see is all the rings together. You can swipe to see each ring individually.

At any time, you can change your goals by opening the app, then pressing firmly on the display. You can also have reminders sent to you to encourage you to complete your goal.

In the Activity app on your iPhone, you can view your Activity history, and see more detailed reports about what you've done. The measurements will get more accurate as you wear the watch more, and it gets to know your behaviors.

# Workout

Workout is kind of a companion to Activity even though there's a separate app for it. The point of it is to help you track progress during a workout session and help you hit new milestones.

From your Home screen, tap the Workout app and you'll immediately see dozens of different workouts. They range from brisk walks to more intense workouts—both indoor and outdoor. For indoor and outdoor running or walking and outdoor cycling, you can also set a distance goal. You can also choose no goal and simply get started.

Once you hit Begin, the watch will immediately count down to the start. During your workout, a ring will steadily fill in here as you approach your goal.

To pause or end the workout, just press firmly on the display and press End or Pause. When you end the workout, you can scroll through a full summary. You can either save the data or discard it.

## Check Your Heart Rate

To get the best results with your heart rate, make sure the watch is tight enough to touch the skin, but not too tight. From your watch face, swipe up and go to the Heartbeat glance; next tap the heart to take a reading.

If you are in a workout, you can check your heart rate by swiping on the lower half of the Workout progress screen.

## Set Alarms

If you want to set an alarm, go to the Alarm Clock app from your watch's home screen. Once it's open, press firmly on the display, then tap New +. Tap Change Time (remember to also change AM / PM); you can use the Digital Crown knob to adjust the hours and minutes. Finally tap Set. You can tap the < in the upper left corner to return to the alarm settings, where you can repeat an alarm, push snooze, or label it.

To adjust an alarm, tap the Alarm Clock app, then tap the alarm in the list that you want to change. Tap next to the alarm to turn it on or off. You can delete an alarm by tapping on then alarm, then scrolling to the bottom and tapping Delete.

## Use a Timer

To use the watch's timer, go to the home screen and tap Timer; timers can be set for up to 24 hours. To set a timer, open the app, tap hours or minutes, turn the Digital Crown knob to adjust the time, and finally tap Start. If the timer will be more than 12 hours, then while adjusting the timer press firmly on the display and tap 0-24 hours.

## Use the Stopwatch

If you want to use the stopwatch to time things like the time of a track lap, then go to your home screen and tap Stopwatch app. To start the watch, tap the Start button; tap the lap button to split the time or record a lap. Timing will continue as you switch between them. When you are finished, tap Reset.

You can also pick the format for the stopwatch; there are four different ones: Analog, Digital, Graph, and Hybrid.

# Remote Control

A lesser-known fact about the watch is that it doubles as a remote control iTunes and Apple TV.

Before you begin make sure both your watch and your device are using the same network; if your phone is using one Wi-Fi and your watch is using another, then they won't work.

### *Remote Play iTunes*

If you'd like to use the watch as a remote for iTunes on your Mac, open up the Remote app; next tap the Add Device+.

In iTunes on your computer, click the Remote button near the top of the iTunes window; it will ask you to enter the 4-digit code that is now displayed on your watch. (Note: if you look for the Remote button in iTunes before you tap Add Device on the Apple Watch, you'll be waiting a long time—it will only appear after you tap Add Device; also make sure iTunes is up-to-date.)

## *Remote for Apple TV*

If you'd like to use the watch as a remote for iTunes on your Apple TV, open up the Remote app; next tap the Add Device+. (Note: remember you must be using the same Wi-Fi Network.)

On your Apple TV go to Settings, and then General, and finally Remote, and select the Apple Watch; enter the passcode that's currently on your watch.

# Accessibility and Other Features

Like every Apple product, the Apple Watch has accessibility features to help people with disabilities.

It works very similar to your iPhone; to access the features, go to the Apple Watch app on your iPhone, then My Watch, then General, and finally Accessibility.

## VoiceOver

VoiceOver helps you use the watch even if you can't see the watch. It will read back everything that's on the watch for you. You can turn it on by going to the Settings app on the watch's home screen, then General, Accessibility, and finally VoiceOver.

When VoiceOver is on, you can move your finger around the display and listen to the name of each item you touched. VoiceOver also uses different gestures; you can go back by using two fingers to draw a "Z" shape on the display. To open an app, you will double tap it instead of single tap. To pause the VoiceOver from reading what's on the screen, tap the display with two fingers; tap with two fingers again to resume play.

When you set up your watch for the first time, you can use VoiceOver as well. When you turn on the watch for the first time, press the side button; after it turns on, triple click the Digital Crown knob.

## Zoom

The watch is a small display—perhaps even smaller than you thought it would be—so it's understandable that you might want the display a little bigger. If that's the case, go to the Settings app, and then turn on General, Accessibility, and Zoom.

To zoom in or out when Zoom is enabled you will double-tap the display with two fingers. To move around (or pan) the display, you will drag with two fingers.

## Bold Text

Putting the text in boldface is another way to make reading the text on your screen a little easier. You can make the text boldface by going to the Settings app on your home screen, then tapping General and Accessibility and turning on Bold Text; the watch will need to be restarted before this goes into effect.

# Handling

## Removing the Bands

To change a band, press the band release button on the Apple Watch, and slide the band across, then slide in the new band. You should never force a band into the slot, as this could get it stuck.

It is recommended that you fit the band so it is close to your skin, but not so tight that it is squeezing your wrist.

## Band Care

Apple recommends that you clean the leather portions of bands with a nonabrasive, lint-free cloth that is, if necessary, dampened with water. The band should not be attached to the watch. After cleaning, let the band dry before reattaching to the watch. Do not store leather in direct sunlight or in high temperatures or high humidity; you also should not soak the leather in water as it is not water resistant.

For all other bands, Apple recommends cleaning the same way, but the band should be dried with a nonabrasive, lint-free cloth.

# Other Topics

## Force Restarting the Apple Watch

In very rare cases, the Apple Watch may freeze or need to be force restarted. If this ever happens, hold down the side button and Digital Crown knob at the same time for ten seconds. When the Apple Logo appears, you can let go.

## Resetting the Watch Settings

If you want to reset the watch settings and make the watch new (remember this erases everything) then go to the Settings app from the Home screen, then go to General, Reset, and finally Erase All Content and Settings. Once it's reset you will need to pair it with your phone again. Make sure you do this if you ever sell or give your watch or phone away, as your vital information (like credit cards) will be available to that person if you don't.

## Get Your Watch DNA

If you need to know what model number your watch is, what software version it is, what its serial number is, or what its capacity is then go to the Settings app from your Home screen, and then General and About.

## Update Apple Watch Software

Much like the iPhone and iPad, updates to the Apple Watch software are done over the air—meaning you won't need to plug anything in.

To see if there's an update, open the Apple Watch app on the iPhone, then tap My Watch, General, and finally Software Updates. It will tell you if there's an update, and then you just follow the steps. Updates don't happen very often—usually just a handful of times each year.

# Watch Bands & Accessories

What's a watch without its band? Unlike traditional bands, the Apple Watch makes it remarkably easy to switch out bands. And unlike any other Apple product, you have *lots* of options; normally an Apple product comes in two or three colors; with the watches there are several dozen ways to mix and match.

Below is a guide to all the different ones you have to choose from. (Note: when purchasing a band, remember that a 42mm band won't be compatible with a 38mm band or vice versa). Unless otherwise noted, all bands are available in both 38 and 42mm. Some bands are not one size fits all.

## Official Bands & Accessories

Sport Band ($49)

It's available in black, space gray, white, pink, blue, green. The band is obviously best for working out; it's also the cheapest band available. It's made of fluoroelastomer, a synthetic rubber known for performing well in heat. Because this band isn't one size fits all, the chart below helps you make the right choice:

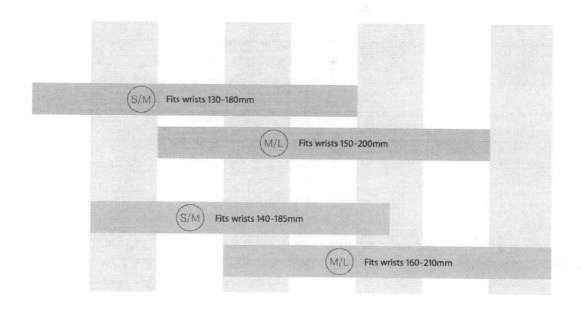

S/M Fits wrists 130-180mm

M/L Fits wrists 150-200mm

S/M Fits wrists 140-185mm

M/L Fits wrists 160-210mm

Classic Buckle ($149)

This band is made of "Dutch leather" from a tannery in the Netherlands. Apple promises the mill gives it a distinctive texture. The closer is made of stainless steel.

Milanese Loop ($149)

Apple says the inspiration for this stainless steel mesh band was a mesh band from 19th century Milan. The band is completely magnetic and easy to put on.

Modern Buckle ($249) - three sizes: small, medium, and large

It's available in brown, black, pink, and midnight blue. The leather for this stunning band comes from a French tannery established in 1803. How are the modern and classic bands different? The leather is slightly different, but the most noticeable difference is the buckle. The classic is a strap with holes; the modern is a magnetic band that helps you have a more precise fit. Because this band isn't one size fits all, the chart below helps you make the right choice:

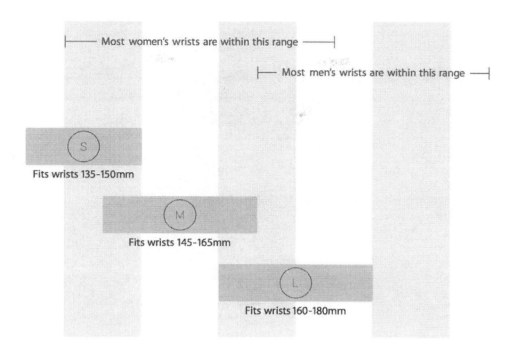

Most women's wrists are within this range

Most men's wrists are within this range

S
Fits wrists 135-150mm

M
Fits wrists 145-165mm

L
Fits wrists 160-180mm

Link Bracelet ($449.00)

The most expensive and complex band, this stainless steel band has over 100 parts. Apple claims the craftsmanship is so complex that it takes nine hours to assemble a single case. The magnetic closure is one size fits all.

Leather Loop ($149) - Only available for the 42mm band.

It's available in stone, light brown, bright blue, and black. Made of Venezia leather and handcrafted in Arzignano, Italy, this band has a soft and gilded feel. The magnetic loop is easy to put on. Because this band isn't one size fits all, the chart below helps you make the right choice:

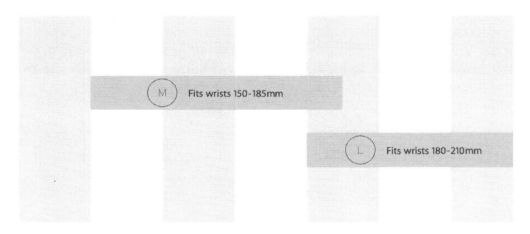

Apple Watch Magnetic Charging Cable ($29 for 1m cable; $39 for 2m cable)

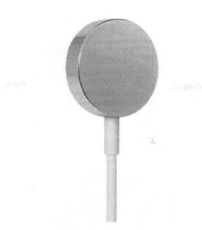

Apple has only announced one official accessory for the Apple Watch, and that is an extra charger (one comes free with your watch).

# Unofficial Bands

There's no denying the Apple Watch bands are slick…but they're also expensive. If you want to complement your watch with something a little less pricey, lots of options have already popped up, and many more are coming.

Casetify (<u>www.casetify.com/apple-watch</u>)

Click has a collection of bands for $50. For the same price, you can also customize your band and add your own photos for a truly unique fashion statement.

Click (https://www.get-click.com/)

Click is a $10 component that attaches to your Apple Watch and lets you and any band you want--so if you have a nice traditional band in your closet, this is a great option for you.

Monowear Design (www.monoweardesign.com)

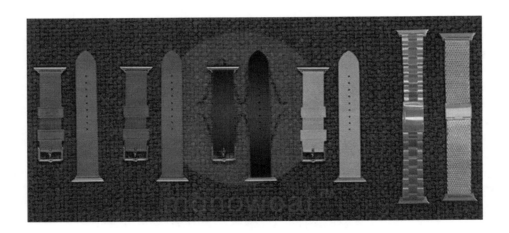

Monowear Design promises to have Apple style for not Apple prices. A leather or linked band that looks surprisingly similar to Apple's bands can be purchased for less than $100.

Reserve Strap (www.reservestrap.com)

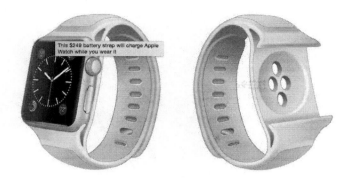

If you are worried about battery usage on the Apple Watch, then Reserve Watch might be for you. The $249.99 promises to give your watch more juice (no mention of how much at this writing). This watch is currently available for pre-order, but it's not yet known when the band will be released.

Pod by Nomad ([www.hellonomad.com/products/pod-for-apple-watch](www.hellonomad.com/products/pod-for-apple-watch))

For people wanting to charge their watch on the go without the $249 band strap price tag, there's also the Pod by Nomad, which is priced at $59.95. This small device can easily fit in purse or briefcases, and promises to charge your watch four times before needing a recharge itself.

X-doria (shop.x-doria.com/)

There are already several bumper guards for the Apple Watch (which help shield your watch from scratches much like a case). One is the $29.99 Defense Edge.

Var Cyclip (http://www.thecyclip.com/)

The Var Cyclip promises to be perhaps the first accessory that lets you attach your watch to a handlebar (whether bike, moped, or motorcycle). No word at this writing about the price or availability.

Calypso Timeless (https://www.calypsocrystal.com)

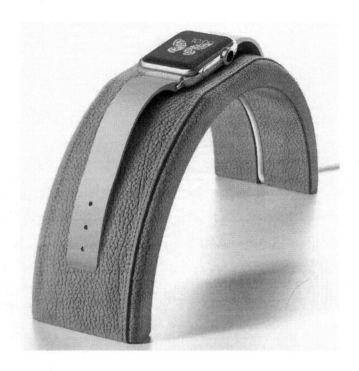

You paid a lot for your watch, so why not show it off? If you want a classy stand for your watch, check out the Calypso Timeless -- a $129 stand.

These are some of the many bands available, but look for hundreds of other options as months go by.

# Understanding Warranty and AppleCare

Because of how delicate the watch can be it's important to understand what's covered and what's not covered under the watch warranty.

## Covered

Debris under the display glass or pixel anomaly; the back cover is removed but there is no damage (by damage, there should be absolutely no evidence that the cover was removed by prying); and finally, condensation in the heart rate sensor windows.

## Covered With Fees

Damages that are covered out-of-warranty include cracked, missing, removed, or damaged Digital Crown cap; abrasions, puncture holes, missing buttons from a drop, chips in the display, a removed back cover with damage, a bent band enclosure, a missing band release, or any cracks on the back cover.

Fees do apply to these services, and the cost depend on the model and if you have AppleCare +.

## Ineligible for Service

The following damages are considered ineligible for warranty services: disassembling unit or missing parts, catastrophic damage, counterfeit or third-part parts, and lastly unauthorized modifications. (Note: catastrophic damage may be covered with AppleCare+; check with the Apple Store and explain the situation; it's provided at their discretion).

Apple disclosed earlier this month that it will charge out-of-warranty service fees of $229, $329 and $2,800 for the Sport, Watch and Edition models respectively for repairs not covered by Apple's limited one-year warranty or AppleCare+ for Apple Watch. Out-of-warranty battery service is also available for $79 plus an applicable $6.95 shipping charge if required for all

Apple Watch models.

# AppleCare

Every Apple Watch does come with AppleCare; for extended service, however, AppleCare also offers AppleCare+.

What's the difference? The free level care includes a one year limited warranty for hardware repairs and 90 days of free technical support. AppleCare+ extends the warranty for two years. For the pricier Apple Watch Edition, this warranty is extended an additional year. With AppleCare+ you get two incidences of accidental damage (fees do apply).

Before paying for AppleCare, one thing you should consider doing is checking the services your credit card offers; some credit cards will offer warranty extensions if you use their card for purchase. Some even consider loss or theft (which, by the way, AppleCare+ does not cover).

So is AppleCare+ worth it? Personally, I like it for peace of mind; I don't have to worry about expensive cases or banging the watch on something. Apple Stores have terrific customer support when it comes to AppleCare+.

As companies learn about what makes the watch tick, then services are bound to pop up that offer repairs more cheaply than what AppleCare charges, but Apple will always be the simplest way to repair your watch.

# Appendix: The Apps

## Apple Apps

This book has covered all the apps already on the phone, but for a quick overview, here they are again.

- Messages - This is where you will send and receive text messages (and also send and receive animated emojis).
- Phone - This is, obviously, where you make and receive calls, but it should be noted that when you are using the phone on your wrist, you can also transfer that call to your iPhone, so if you step into a place where speakerphone is frowned upon, you don't have to hang up and call back.
- Mail - You can read your mail message, but it's not for replying--it's more for managing mail (i.e., deleting, reading, flagging, and moving).
- Calendar - this app lets you quickly browse through your calendar and also accept and decline invitations.
- Activity -- this app is a bit of motivational workout app--it gives you a summary of how much you are standing, exercising, moving...in short it makes you feel guilty about how lazy you are.
- Workout -- when you are working out, you tell your watch what you are doing (running, walking, cycling) and then it shows you how far you've gone, and how fast you are going.
- Maps -- a turn-by-turn map...with a twist--when it's time for you to turn, it taps you on the wrist.
- Passbook - This is essentially a micro version of Passbook for the iPhone, but instead of holding your phone to the scanner, you hold your wrist.
- Siri - Siri is one of the most important apps on the Apple Watch because with no keyboard, you need it to find things quickly; to use it, just lift your wrist and say "Hey Siri"--no buttons need to be pressed to bring up Siri.
- Music- The music app is what you'd expect...unless you expect to plug in headsets; there's no audio input on the watch so you have to use Bluetooth headphones to listen.
- Camera Remote - The watch has no built in camera; what it has in its place is a viewfinder, so if you want to take a selfie with your phone then you can use the watch to take the photo.
- Remote - If you have an Apple TV, this app lets you control it from your wrist; you can also use it to control your Mac or PC's iTunes library.
- Weather - Lets you see a visual summary of weather where you are or anywhere else in the world.

- Stocks - With this app you can see stock performance for up to six months.
- Photos - This is where you will view all your favorite photos.
- Alarm / Stopwatch / Timer - These are three relatively simple apps that do exactly what you'd expect them to do.
- World Clock - while the watch's time face screen is the main feature, it does have a second app for tracking time around the world.
- Settings - This is where you can turn off Wi-Fi, Bluetooth, etc.

# Non-Apple Apps

Chances are you've heard about all the popular apps for the Apple Watch already. I'm talking about Twitter, Instagram, etc. So below, I'm putting some of my favorite apps that you might not have heard of.

SwipeSpeare

SwipeSpeare puts Shakespeare's words into modern English with a swipe; when you launch the app, you pick your play and then you are asked if you want to read it in modern English or the original language. Any time you want to see what the passage says in the other translation, you just swipe your finger across the passage. It includes a free copy of Romeo and Juliet too! The watch app syncs your notes, bookmarks, and highlights.

SwipeBible

There aren't a lot of Bible apps for the watch yet. You probably know about all the popular ones, but one you might not have heard of is SwipeBible; it's from the makers of SwipeSpeare and it's entirely free. It lets you open up to nine Bible translations at the same time and toggle between the translations by swiping over the verse. The companion app is much like SwipeSpeare and lets you manage notes, bookmarks, and highlights.

Do Button

Always forgetting to do things like turning off the lights? Try this app, which helps keep your life a little more organized.

## Dating

Your love life is now on your phone. Two popular dating apps (OkCupid and Match Dating App) have already figured out a way to put your dating life on your wrist. Looking for love? Try these apps!

## Games

Games are not ideal for Apple Watch; however, a few have already figured out how to do it. One is BoxPop, which is both challenging and addicting. Word games are also a great fit; one word game that has already figure out how to make a nice game for the wrist is Letter Zap.

## PowerPoint

Apple has, of course, promoted their own software's app: Keynote. Not as much attention has been given to PowerPoint; the Microsoft app lets you use your watch as a remote to your PowerPoint slides on your iPhone.

## CALC

Calculator is more than a calculator app; it also lets you figure out how much to tip at a restaurant. It's easy to use and pretty powerful for a watch app. It's free to download and $1.99 for premium features. If all you want to do is tip, then another nice app is Cow Tipper.

## Tasty Recipes

Reading is not always easy on the watch; while I don't recommend reading a book on the watch, recipes are a perfect fit; this lets you leave your watch in another room while making all your favorite dishes by giving you a step-by-step guide right on your watch.

## The Johnson & Johnson Official 7 Minute Workout

Apple has you covered with a great workout app—but if you want to change it up a little, or just looking for something that gets you exercised a little…quicker—then try this app. As the name implies it gives you an intense workout in just seven minutes.

Day One

Writing is not what the watch was made for—so a journal app (priced at $4.99) seems like an odd thing to make an app for; still, this app is surprisingly intuitive and easy to use. You can make quick notes about where you are or use the watch's Mic to include writing.

Made in the USA
San Bernardino, CA
03 December 2016